# TABLE SETTING GUIDE

## By SHARON DLUGOSCH

BRIGHTON PUBLICATIONS, INC.

# BRIGHTON PUBLICATIONS, INC.

Illustrations by Sandra Knuth

Copyright © by Sharon E. Dlugosch

Brighton Publications, Inc.
P.O. Box 12706
New Brighton, MN 55112
(612)636-2220

Revised Edition: 1990

Library of Congress Cataloging-in-Publication Data

Dlugosch, Sharon.
    Table setting guide.

    Includes index.
    1. Table setting and decoration.      I. Title.
TX873.D58    1990          642′.6          90-2353
          ISBN 0-918420-11-3

Printed in the United States of America

To my children, Janice,
Christine, and Brian.

A special thank you to Florence Nelson, for her expert advice and to my mother Did Haberman and my husband, Jim, for their support.

# CONTENTS

# Basic Table Service

## Table Service

Table service describes how to serve food to guests or family. The activity includes setting the table, placing the food on the table, offering the food to the people who are to be served and the removal of food and dishes. Table service can be elaborate or simply functional as the occasion or setting demands. Recently, we have seen a trend away from formal manners reserved for guests and a more relaxed way of serving and eating food that can be shared by family and guests alike. The following five patterns of table service are used most often in homes today.

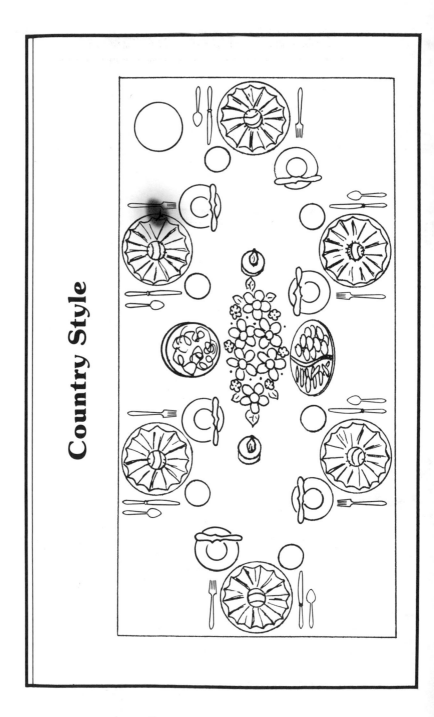

Country Style

# Basic Table Service

**COUNTRY STYLE SERVICE** is preferred for serving large groups of people in a short time and reduces the chance of cold food. To save time, place all the serving dishes on the table before the family is seated. If the table becomes too crowded, place some of the serving dishes on a tea cart or small table.

## UNIQUE FEATURES

- Requires a large enough table to accommodate serving dishes and an area large enough for the table.
- The table is completely set and serving dishes are placed at intervals on the table.
- Each dish is taken by the nearest person and passed from hand to hand. To reduce confusion always serve in one direction.
- Table waiting is done by one or more members of the group who remove the main course and serve the dessert course.

*Serve from the left side, clear from the right side except when serving beverages.*

# Family Service

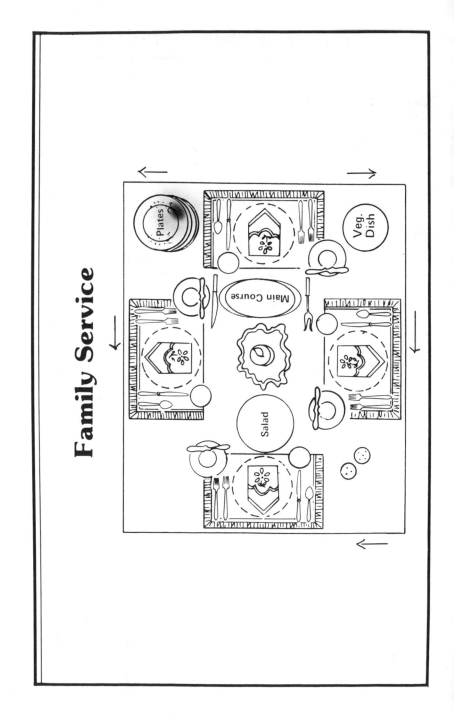

# Basic Table Service

**FAMILY SERVICE** most resembles yesterday's formal dining. Instead of servants, family members contribute to the serving of food. Usually two people at opposite ends of the table serve the individual portions and pass the plate to each person until all have been served. Use family service when the number of people at the table is small to avoid the problem of cold food because of length of serving time. This service does provide a feeling of togetherness in an otherwise crowded day.

## UNIQUE FEATURES

- Requires dining table and dining area.
- Family members perform serving duties.
- At least one course is served at the table.
- All portions to be eaten from the main plate are carved and served from one end of the table and plates are passed in order to each side of the table.
- If help is necessary, the person sitting on the left of the main course may help serve the vegetable, gravy or any other dish.
- The person seated at the opposite end of the table may toss and serve the salad. Beverage and dessert is also served by this person.
- Beverage and dessert may be brought from the kitchen or may be served at the table.
- After the main course has been served the relish, rolls or other food may be passed around.

*Try this service for those occasional unhurried meals.*

## Apartment Service

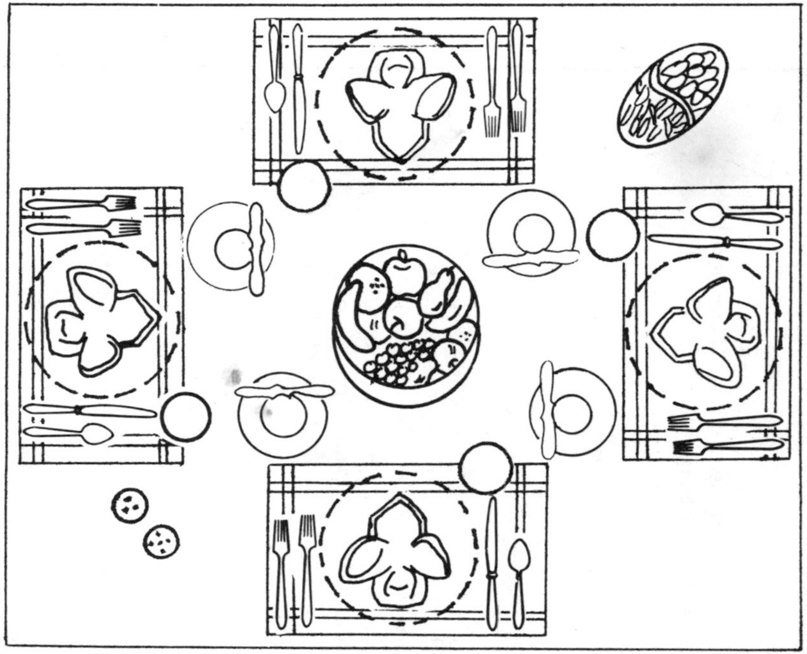

# Basic Table Service

**APARTMENT SERVICE** fulfills the need of hospitality when the convenience of a large dining area or table is missing. This service is also handy when there are small children in the family. Each child is sure to receive a portion of food and this eliminates the chance of accidents caused by tiny hands.

This pattern of service is also known as blue-plate service. If there is help in the kitchen, more than six to eight people may be served by this method.

Because the serving dishes are placed on an end table or serving cart, smaller pieces of furniture such as a desk or coffee table may be pressed into use as a dining table.

## UNIQUE FEATURES

- Requires a small group of six to eight people because of time consuming dishing up of food.
- Plates are dished out in the kitchen and placed on the table immediately before guests sit down.
- Any course before the main course of the meal (appetizer) is served before group comes to the table.
- Serving dishes may be placed on an end table or serving cart.
- Removal of main course and serving dessert may be done by one of the group.

*Use apartment service to entertain small groups in less than adequate dining areas.*

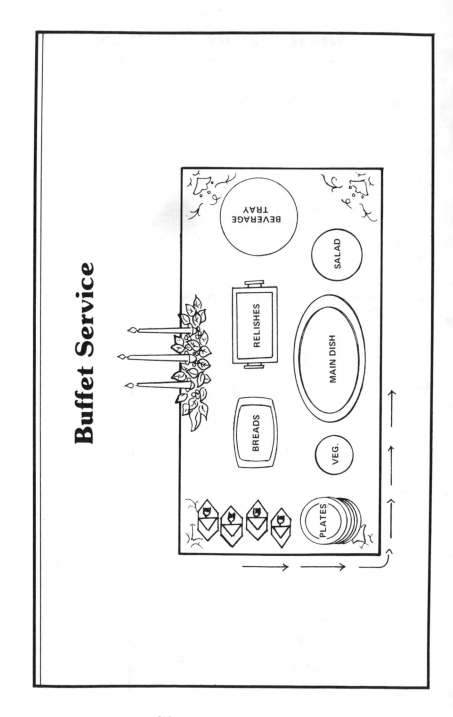

# Buffet Service

# Basic Table Service

**BUFFET SERVICE** is convenient for large groups of people in a small home. However, the menu should be planned carefully for this style of serving. If guests are standing, the menu should not include food which must be cut by a knife. The serving dishes and appointments should also be planned carefully for optimum convenience. Fold napkins into a package like the Diagonal Buffet Fold* and place flatware inside.

## UNIQUE FEATURES

- Requires a table or any suitable surface such as a chest, desk, serving table or kitchen counter which may be used for the service plates.
- Card tables or a small dining table may be completely set with all the appointments needed. Seating may be at card tables or a small dining table.
- Guests may also be provided with trays for their plate and beverage.
- If guests must stand, provide plenty of space to set beverages while they eat from their hand-held plate.
- Guests may also be expected to stand while eating at large receptions.

*Combine buffet serving with a tastefully set dining table for an elegant but easy dinner party.*

* *"Folding Table Napkins: A New Look At A Traditional Craft," by Sharon Dlugosch, Brighton Publications.*

# Table Setting Guide

**TEA SERVICE** is appropriate for large receptions or small dessert parties.

## UNIQUE FEATURES

- Requires tray or table for appointments.
- Service may be from either end of the table or from one side.
- Table may be dining table, card table, lamp table or other small table.
- Beverage may be correctly received first or last.
- Use tea size (about 12 inches square) napkins.
- Provide a plate or saucer for beverage if finger food is served. This allows a container for the food and frees the right hand for eating.
- Food requiring flatware should be served on a plate. The beverage should be in a cup and placed either on the plate or a saucer.

## Tea Service

*Plan dessert parties as an easy, informal alternative to dinner parties.*

# Basic Table Service

## Table Service

On most informal occasions, when just the family is present, meals are usually one course without the need for table service. In a more formal occasion, especially if guests are present, it is appropriate for a family member to wait on the table. Use a nearby buffet or serving cart to help facilitate serving and removal.

Removal of the main course begins with serving dishes after which, the plates and individual casseroles, if used, may be removed. Use a small tray to pick up any flatware not used and other small objects. Placing a cloth or paper napkin on the tray will cut down on extra noise.

Serving a course is just the opposite sequence. Begin with placing the flatware at each place setting and bringing any dishes that may be needed. Finally, bring in the food.

The bread and butter plate, the salad plate and the dinner plate should be placed on the table or removed from the left side of the place setting. Pick up with the left hand and transfer to the right hand. Flatware on the left of the place setting should be removed from the left also. Glassware, cups and flatware on the right side of the place setting should be served or removed with the right hand. Refill glasses from the right side. Do not lift glasses to fill them. Slide them to the edge of the table if necessary.

*Use left arm to serve from left side.*

17

# Table Setting Guide

## Table Service Terms

1. The term "covers" describe individual place settings including dinnerware, glasses, flatware and linens.

2. "Underliner" is a plate used under another plate, an appetizer dish or glass, an individual casserole or soup bowl. The spoon when not in use is placed on the underliner. Use the underliner for a more attractive table setting or for easier handling. Flatware used with this course is placed on the underliner to the side of the dish or glass.

3. "FRENCH SERVICE," or serving from a platter, uses a spoon-and-fork combination in one hand as though it were a set of tongs. This service is most often seen in luxury restaurants.

# Setting The Table

## Placing the Tablecovers and Linens

1. Tablecloths should be sized to the table allowing about a 15-inch drop on each side. The center fold, the only allowed crease in the cloth, should rest exactly at center of table.

2. Rectangular place mats may be placed flush with the table edge or one to one and one-half inches from the edge.

3. Place rectangular mats on a round or oval table so that the points are touching the edges.

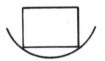

4. Round mats may lay at edge of round table. Mats may also drape over the rectangular or round table.

5. Runners can be placed at center of table or at each edge of a narrow table. Overhang should be about 15 inches.

6. Napkins may be placed at the left of place settings or folded and placed on the bread and butter plate, main plate or arranged in glass.

## Placing the Dinnerware

1. The salad plate may be placed at the top of the fork. If a bread and butter plate is used, set this plate above the fork and the salad plate below and to the left. Or the salad plate may be above the main plate. Since using both salad and bread and butter plate may crowd the small table, it is best to omit the bread and butter plate.

# Table Setting Guide

2. Individual casseroles placed on a liner (salad plate or pie plate) are positioned above the plate. The serving spoon may be placed with the other flatware at the place setting or beside the casserole.

3. Coffee cups, if used with the main meal, are set with the top of the saucer forming a straight line with the top of the last piece of flatware on the right. Position the cup so the handle is at the right to make it easier to grasp with the right hand.

# Laying the Flatware

1. Flatware is placed on the table in the order of need, starting from the outside of the place setting.

2. Knives are placed next to the plate with the cutting edge towards the plate.

3. Spoons are placed with the bowls facing up at the right of the knife. Placing the spoon bowls and fork tines down is a continental way of setting the table still used in many French homes.

4. Lay the dinner fork next to the plate and the salad fork to the left if the salad is to be eaten before the main course. If the salad is to be eaten with the main course or after, place the salad fork next to the plate.

5. If the bread and butter plate is used, lay the butter spreader across the top edge of the plate, parallel to the table or across the right side of the plate with curved edge of blade toward the left. You may omit the butter spreader if the table knife is included in the place setting.

# Setting The Table

6. Flatware for dessert may be placed above the plate with handles toward the right or brought to the table at the same time dessert is served.

7. When eating fresh fruits, place the fruit knife with handle toward the right and the fork below, with handle toward the left above the main plate. If a beverage spoon is used for dessert, place this above the knife with handle towards the right.

8. If a serving tray of fruit is used, place the fruit knives together on the same tray for the guests who decide to use a knife.

9. The flatware for eating cheese and crackers may also be arranged above the main plate.

10. Arrange the flatware handles in an even line with the edge of the plate for a pleasing unbroken line.

# Placing the Glassware

1. Place water glass at or near tip of knife.

2. If milk glasses are used, place glass to the right of the water glass and a little closer to table edge. If just milk is served, place glass at tip of knife.

3. Juice is sometimes served on a small plate at the center of the place setting for a more formal service. Otherwise place juice glass a little closer to the edge of the table from the last glass.

4. Set an iced tea or coffee glass on a small plate to provide a place to rest the spoon if sugar is used.

# Table Setting Guide

5. Place wine glasses to the right of the water glass and closer to the edge of the table.

# Table Decorating

1. Candles, if used, should either be lower or higher than eye level in order to keep the flame from distracting the guests.

2. Use fresh fruits and vegetables as decorations, keying color to the theme and season.

3. For warm and personal centerpieces, use items from a hobby, such as a rock or shell collection.

4. To save space in small apartments push the table against a wall and hang an appropriate picture, providing decoration for the table without using table space.

5. Arrange colorful maps and flags of destination for a bon voyage party.

6. Dress up Christmas cookie cutters with calico ribbon pasted to the sides; hang cookie cutters on a mug holder stand. Extra cookie cutters can be used as napkin rings.

7. Use small brown paper bags with votive candles stuck into sand for a Mexican fiesta party.

# Setting The Table

8. Try this space-saving idea for your crowded buffet table . . . wicker hanging baskets filled with flowers or ivy. Lets baskets hang at eye level above buffet table.

9. Scrape out a large squash such as Hubbard for a Thanksgiving cornucopia. Fill with an assortment of fruit and vegetables.

10. Use candles in stemmed glasses; different heights add to the attraction. Drip a little of the melting wax in the bottom of the glass and press candle down. Candles without perfume will blend best with your menu.

11. Cut lemons into thin rounds. Secure rounds on wooden picks, place in frog. Fill in with vegetable greens and flowers.

12. Gather the group together from your last vacation trip for a memory party. Build a "house of cards" with photos and postcards.

13. For an Italian pasta eating experience try varying lengths of spaghetti tucked in a straw basket with a floral centerpiece. Add Italy's tricolors: red, white and green ribbons.

*more themes and ideas...*

# Table Setting Guide

*Dates to remember...*

## Traditional Anniversary Gift List

| | |
|---|---|
| 1. Paper | 13. Lace |
| 2. Cotton | 14. Ivory |
| 3. Leather | 15. Crystal |
| 4. Silk | 20. China |
| 5. Wood | 25. Silver |
| 6. Iron | 30. Pearls |
| 7. Copper or wool | 35. Coral and Jade |
| 8. Electric appliances | 40. Ruby |
| 9. Pottery | 45. Sapphire |
| 10. Tin | 50. Gold |
| 11. Steel | 60. Diamond |
| 12. Linen | |

The Traditional Anniversary Gift List suggests themes for your special anniversary dinner. Try these ideas for your next celebration.

**FIRST ANNIVERSARY — PAPER.** Enlarge on the paper theme with gaily colored paper plates and napkins for a fun-filled first anniversary party. Combine paper flowers and streamers for the centerpiece and fold the paper napkins into Mexican Fan Folds (directions found in FOLDING TABLE NAPKINS).

**FIFTH ANNIVERSARY — WOOD.** Tie calico ribbon bows around different sized wooden spoons and stand upright in a wooden bowl or ceramic pot. Make the centerpiece fit the occasion

24

# Setting The Table

by painting the date and names of the anniversary on the bowl of each spoon. At the end of the party the celebrants will have a memento of the occasion.

**TENTH ANNIVERSARY — TIN.** Simply place a candle inside a tin hand grater and place on center of table. The pierced openings will allow the light to flicker through. Continue to carry out the theme with small tin nutmeg graters stuffed with violets or other small flowers at each place setting.

**FIFTEENTH ANNIVERSARY — CRYSTAL.** Set crystal or blown glass figures (perhaps swans) on a square of mirror. Add a few white votive candles for extra reflection from the mirror. Crystal glassware will emphasize the theme and add a sparkling touch to the table setting.

**TWENTY-FIFTH ANNIVERSARY — SILVER.** Run a wide silver ribbon down the length of a white tablecloth and place white candles at intervals on the ribbon. Arrange white flowers in a silver bowl or container; set in center. Shape the number twenty-five with florist wire and wrap tin foil around the wire. Place miniature numbers next to the place cards or make one large twenty-five and tuck into the flower arrangement. Use all the silver serving pieces you can find.

**FIFTIETH ANNIVERSARY — GOLD.** Cover the table with a white tablecloth flecked with gold threads. Make two or three paper fans out of gold wallpaper or wrapping paper and arrange with white ceramic cupids, love birds etc. around a single white candle; place on center of table. Use white, lace trimmed napkins folded in the Cascade Fold (directions found in FOLDING TABLE NAPKINS) and tuck a small gold remembrance into each napkin fold. Beg or borrow gold trimmed dinnerware and gold plated flatware to complement the golden anniversary theme.

# Selection and Easy Care

## Dinnerware

Ttrying to make the best judgement in purchasing dinnerware can be a bewildering experience. One quickly discovers phrases such as "fine china and casual dinnerware" or "hard-as-porcelain stoneware." These phrases are meaningless unless it is known that the term "fine china" includes china, porcelain, bone china and ceramic china, all of which are very durable and also expensive. On the other hand, stoneware is a high quality earthenware used as casual dinnerware. Stoneware is porous and not as durable as china even though some stoneware is advertised as chip and scratch resistant, which is more like the qualities of fine china.

In order to really read the ads and understand the salesperson, it is important to sort kinds of dinnerware into categories, including their characteristics and design.

The choice is yours, ranging from elegant durable translucent china to casual earthenware, some of which is oven and dishwasher proof and suitable for microwaves.

Holloware is the term for all sterling or silver plated serving and decorative items that add to the ease of service and total look of the table. Tea and coffee pots, creamers, sugar bowls, and vegetable dishes, flat dishes and trays are included under the same definition.

# Table Setting Guide

## Selection of Dinnerware

*Purchasing dinnerware varies within a wide range of price. Many people begin dinnerware buying with:*

**OPEN STOCK**, which allows the purchase of individual dishes or by the dozen. Usually open stock will be available for only from five to ten years. To promote sales some companies are guaranteeing a 25-year replacement.

**STARTER SET** may have as few as 16 pieces: four dinner plates, four bread and butter plates, four cups and four saucers. Pieces can be added as they're needed.

**PLACE SETTING** is a complete service for one person and generally includes dinner plate, dessert or salad plate, cup and saucer, and bread and butter plate. The soup dish may be added to this service. Start with two placesettings and add pieces as you need them, including serving dishes, sugar and cream set and other pieces.

## Before You Purchase

Consider these points when purchasing your casual dinnerware or fine china.
- Country of origin.
- Name of manufacturer.
- Shape of body.
- Breakage warranty.
- Pattern or design.
- Price.

# Selection and Easy Care

## Buying Dishes by the Set

*my favorite patterns...*

Service for 4
4 dinner plates 10″
4 salad 8″
4 bread & butter
4 cups
4 saucers


Service for 8
8 dinner plates
8 salad
8 bread & butter
8 cups
8 saucers
1 creamer
1 sugar bowl
1 sugar bowl lid
1 platter
1 vegetable dish

# Table Setting Guide

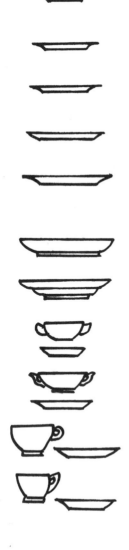

## Dinnerware Pieces

**Bread-and-Butter Plate:** six-inch plate (in diameter from edge to edge) for bread, rolls and butter.

**Salad or Pie Plate:** seven-inch plate used for salads or desserts.

**Breakfast or Salad Plate:** eight-inch plate used for breakfast or larger salads.

**Luncheon Plate:** nine-inch plate used for the main course at luncheon.

**Dinner Plate:** ten-inch plate used for the main course.

**Service or Place Plate:** an ornately decorated plate, an inch longer than a dinner plate, used at formal events to hold the container for the first course.

**Coupe Soup:** shallow, flat, round bowl without handles, seven or eight inches in diameter.

**Rimmed Soup:** similar to a coupe soup, but with a rim or shoulder which makes it appear larger.

**Bouillon Cup and Saucer:** two-handled cup, similar to a teacup, used for serving clear soups.

**Cream-Soup Bowl and Saucer:** two-handled low bowl to serve bisques and cream soups at informal meals.

**Teacup and Saucer:** traditional size used for either tea or coffee.

**Demitasse:** small-size cup and saucer for after-dinner coffee.

# Selection and Easy Care

## Design and Decorating

*Design and decorating also enters into the decision of buying dinnerware. Dinnerware designs are classified as to types:*

**IN-THE-CLAY** decorations are designs that are cut or printed on moist clay.

**IN-THE-GLAZE** decorating is done by coloring the glaze itself.

**UNDER-THE-GLAZE** decorations are very durable and smooth to the touch because they are permanent; the glaze goes over the pattern.

**OVER-THE-GLAZE** decorations must be fired on the dishes in decorating ovens so they will last. Gold and platinum are applied over the glaze because they lose their beauty under glaze. Usually there are many colors on the pattern and the design texture is slightly rough in contrast to the rest of the dish, when the pattern is over the glaze. Some dishes use a combination of both methods.

Contemporary design has altered the shapes of dishes (i.e. the rimmed plates or soups). One such design is the coupe shape. Coupe plates or bowls curve up at the edge to form a shallow bowl without a rim. Usually the regular coupe soup bowl is seven or eight inches in diameter.

Cups should be designed deep enough so that the hot beverage will not cool quickly. The handle should be easy to hold.

# Choose Your Dinnerware

## CHINA

| TYPE | CHARACTERISTICS | DISADVANTAGES | PRICE RANGE |
|------|-----------------|---------------|-------------|
| CHINA | Strong. Translucent. Nonporous, won't absorb food or dirt. | Various grades. The thinnest indicates high quality. | Expensive. |
| PORCELAIN | Looks like glass. Very strong. | Not as durable as china. | Expensive. |
| BONE CHINA | Milky-white ware. Strong. Translucent. | Soft glaze which mars easily. | Medium to high. |
| CERAMIC | Nonporous. Translucent. Strong. Ovenproof. Excellent for informal use. | | Less expensive then fine china. |

# EARTHENWARE

| | | |
|---|---|---|
| SEMI-VITREOUS | Opaque. Somewhat porous. Thinner than other types of earthenware but thicker than china. | Shows scratches because of high gloss. May be rather soft. When it chips, it will absorb food and dirt. | Medium. |
| STONEWARE | Nonporous. Heat retentive. Dishwasher safe. Ovenproof (some). Better grade of decorative pottery and tableware. | Doesn't have delicacy, light colors or translucency of china. | Lower to medium. |
| POTTERY | Thick. Heavy to touch. Opaque. Variety of colors, designs and textures. | May not last long in everyday use. Glazes craze from heat and use. Cracked or chipped surface will absorb liquid and food stains. | Low to medium. |

# OTHER DINNERWARE

| | | | |
|---|---|---|---|
| METALS:<br>SILVER<br>PEWTER<br>STAINLESS<br>STEEL | Often used as serving pieces. Stores easily. Regular care with clean warm, mild suds, wipe dry with soft cloth. Unbreakable. Keeps food hot. | Scratches. Silver and pewter tarnish. Water spots. Easily dented. | Medium to high. Silver very expensive. |
| GLASSWARE | Many colors and designs. | Not as versatile as china or earthenware. Easily broken. | Low to high. |
| PLASTIC | Particularly adaptable to casual use. | May crack and stain. Knives sometimes scratch. | Low to medium. |

# Selection and Easy Care

*Quality dinnerware is classified according to condition.*

**SELECTS:** dishes which are perfect.

**RUN-OF-THE-KILN:** dishes which have barely noticeable defects.

**SECOND GRADE:** dishes with noticeable defects but still durable and serviceable.

# Care of Dinnerware

- Scrape with rubber spatula and rinse. Never leave coffee cups unrinsed.

- Avoid temperature changes. Heat china and earthenware in a warm oven only to 150 degrees unless the ware is ovenware.

- Cups should never be stacked inside one another. The overglaze coloring may rub off and handles might break.

- Stand cups separately or hang on hooks.

- When good plates are stacked, place flannel or paper napkin between plates.

- Clean silver serving pieces with a good silver polish.

- Gold linings of pitchers, bowls and salt dishes are delicate; do not rub too hard.

# Terms to Understand for Better Selection of Dinnerware

**BONE CHINA:** China that contains animal bone ash (up to 40 percent) for added translucency and whiteness. Developed originally in England, but now made in Japan and the United States as well.

**CERAMICS:** Pottery, earthenware, china, glass and other products that are made from a mixture of natural materials processed by firing.

**CHINA:** A nonporous type of dinnerware made of white clay and fired at exceptionally high temperature. The finer grades are generally thin, translucent, resistant to chipping, and ring clearly when struck. Some people use this term for all ceramics.

**CRAZING:** Fine cracks appearing in the glaze of dinnerware is known as crazing. It is caused by different rates of expansion between the body and the glaze.

**DELFT:** An earthenware recognized by its blue and white designs. Originally made in Holland and England.

**EARTHENWARE:** A type of clayware that is opaque, somewhat porous, not as strong or as thin as china. It is suitable for everyday use because of its durability, low price, and the variety of available styles. Costly, chip-resistant earthenware is often referred to as fine. The lower grades generally are referred to as coarse.

# Selection and Easy Care

**FINE CHINA:** Thin, translucent china which is very strong, yet very delicate. It is made of top quality clays fired at high temperatures that cause them to fuse into a hard nonporous body.

**GLASS-CERAMIC:** A comparatively new type of dinnerware body that begins as glass, then undergoes special treatment which causes it to take on the appearance of white ceramic. It is very costly, but is the strongest of all dinnerware.

**GLAZE:** A glass-like coating that is applied to pottery and dinnerware by either dipping or spraying. It may be clear or have color. It improves the appearance of dinnerware and makes it moisture-proof as long as the glaze is intact.

**IRONSTONE:** Refers to earthenware of good quality and better than average strength. True Ironstone was originally developed in England. It is thicker and heavier than china, opaque and may absorb moisture when chipped.

**MAJOLICA:** An earthenware that is tin-glazed.

**MELAMINE:** A hard, durable plastic usually found in bright colors for lightweight, inexpensive dinnerware.

**OPAQUE:** Not transparent; an object that blocks all light — cannot be seen through.

**OVENWARE:** Dinnerware that is able to withstand the heat of a kitchen oven without damage. It can be used for both table service and oven cooking. It usually features a casual design with bright colors.

# Table Setting Guide

**PORCELAIN:** A hard, translucent, clayware body that differs very slightly from china in ingredients and manufacturing process. In most respects the two are so much alike that the term can be used interchangeably.

**POTTERY:** A porous and not very durable form of clayware made of crude red or brown clay and fired at comparatively low temperatures.

**SEMI-PORCELAIN:** A type of relatively high-fired, quality earthenware developed in the United States. It is more porous than ironstone.

**STONEWARE:** A hard clayware made of light-colored clay and fired at high temperatures. It is nonporous and very durable, but does not have the translucence of fine china.

**VITRIFIED:** Material that is changed into a glass-like substance by fusion due to heat. This material is nonporous and very hard. All true china is vitrified.

**TRANSLUCENCE:** That quality of fine china that makes it semi-transparent. It may be demonstrated by placing the hand across the back of a piece and holding it up to the light. A silhouette of the hand will be visible through the piece.

# Selection and Easy Care

## Flatware

Choosing flatware requires careful consideration because of the lifetime use good flatware gives. Note the weight and balance of each piece. Is it comfortable held in the hand? If possible, try to arrange a placesetting with the dinnerware and glassware you will be using. This way you can see if the pieces complement each other. Generally the design should coordinate with both casual and fine dinnerware unless two sets of flatware are purchased.

Flatware is commonly sold in sets. The usual choice is the four-piece set which includes luncheon fork and knife, salad fork and teaspoon. The five-piece set includes a cream soup spoon and the six-piece set adds the butter spreader. These basic sets may be added to as the need arises. As you are choosing your starter set, consider buying service pieces such as serving spoons, a salad set, gravy ladle, butter knife and jelly server.

In some cases formal dinners require more than one knife and fork. In that case, a dinner knife and fork, each about three-quarters of an inch longer and proportionately thicker than the luncheon size will be needed.

# Table Setting Guide

## Care of Flatware

- Keep silver flatware clean by using activated charcoal packets in drawer where flatware is stored or by storing silver flatware wrapped in a specially treated cloth called Pacific Cloth.

- Film wrap may also be used to wrap silver pieces to prevent tarnish.

- If silver flatware needs cleaning, use a special silver cleaning product and wipe with long strokes, never circular motions. Rinse article thoroughly before coming in contact with food.

- Wash all flatware as soon as possible after eating.

- Handle a few pieces at a time to minimize scratching, whether washing or putting away in a drawer.

- Check to see if flatware can be put into a dishwasher.

- Keep air out and stored silverware won't tarnish so quickly.

- Enemies of silver are rubber, table salt, eggs, olives, salad dressings, gas, sulfur, vinegar, and fruit juices.

- Pacific Silvercloth keeps silver items clean, bright, and shining, without polishing! Embedded in the cloth are thousands of fine silver particles that absorb tarnish producing gases before they reach the silver. The cloth can be purchased in a 38-inch width and is easy to cut, sew or glue so you can custom design storage pouches, rolls, and liners for drawers or cabinets.

# Choose Your Flatware

## FLATWARE

| TYPE | CHARACTERISTICS | APPEARANCE | PRICE RANGE |
|------|-----------------|------------|-------------|
| STERLING | Composed of 925 parts of pure silver to 75 parts of an alloy, usually copper. Cutting blades are made of high quality stainless steel. The word "sterling" on each piece guarantees the piece as a sterling piece of silver. Sterling lasts a lifetime. | Lustrous dull or mirrorlike finish. | Expensive. |
| SILVERPLATE | Silver is fused electrically over an alloy composed of 65% copper, 17% zinc and 18% nickel. Some pieces are double or triple plated and reinforced at points of greatest wear. | Looks similar to silver in color and surface finish. | Moderate to expensive. |

# FLATWARE

| TYPE | CHARACTERISTICS | APPEARANCE | PRICE RANGE |
|------|-----------------|------------|-------------|
| STAINLESS STEEL | A substance of two or more metals united by being fused together and dissolving in each other when molten. | Soft dull satin finish, slightly burnished or reflective finish. Because of its hardness decoration is kept simple. | Variety of prices. |
| GOLD | 24 karat gold electroplate used with copper or stainless base. Copper base more expensive | Not dishwasher safe. Cannot be used in dishwasher. | Moderate to expensive. |

# Selection and Easy Care

## Additional Notes

- Choose the smaller luncheon forks and knives because they are in scale with most dinnerware and small dining tables.

- Silver and silverplate flatware are buffered and polished either to a bright finish or a softer lustre. Scratches are less noticeable with a softer lustre.

- Knives come with flat or the slightly more expensive hollow handles. Hollow handles are more comfortably gripped but both are equally durable.

- The all-purpose place spoon is a combination of the bouillon spoon, cream soup spoon and dessert spoon which reduces the amount of flatware required for table use.

*My favorite patterns...*

# Table Setting Guide

## Hard-To-Find Flatware Sources

Missing flatware patterns? Don't despair. You may find your hard-to-match or discontinued patterns at the following mail order flatware specialists.

Sterling and silver-plate;
2,400 patterns dating back to 1824.

**Buschemeyer's Jewelers
515 S. Fourth Ave.
Louisville, KY 40202
toll free numbers**
An updated letter sent each month will show inventory and current prices in your pattern. For information send pattern name and manufacturer.

Sterling and silver-plate;
Nearly 50,000 pieces with 2800 patterns inventory.

**Walter Drake Silver Exchange
BR50 Drake Building
Colorado Springs, CO 80940
toll free number: 1-800-525-9826
1-800-523-9827
Colorado residents: 1-800-332-3661**
For information send name of pattern. If you are not sure of pattern ask for the Pattern Directory. It is available at $2.50 (refundable with purchase). A listing of prices and availability of your pattern will be sent.

Sterling only;
Maintains want lists.

**Laurette's Matching Service
2006 Two Tree Lane
Wauwatosa, WI 53213
414-476-8432**
Furnishes fast, personalized service, 10-day return privilege on all silver purchases.

Stainless steel, silverplate, gold plate and sterling made in USA;
115,000 pieces of discontinued patterns.

**Vroman's Silver Shop
1748 So. Grand Ave.
Glendora, CA 91740
213-963-0512**
Send name of pattern, name or symbol of maker, or a Xerox of fork, pieces needed, and type of material. Please include a self-addressed stamped envelope with request.

# Selection and Easy Care

## Glassware

You'll find glassware in sets of four, six, eight, and twelve, category by category. Or you may purchase glassware in sets, like flatware. A basic starter set of glassware includes a water goblet, an all-purpose wine glass and a dessert-champagne. Juice, cocktail, and highball glasses may be added. Often glassware may be purchased individually.

When selecting glassware, check for clarity, sparkle and freedom from bubbles. The tiny bubbles formed in glass when chemicals are united in the fusing or melting of the raw ingredients is known as seed in the glassware industry. No glassware is absolutely free of these tiny specks and they do not constitute defects. Hold the glass and decide if it is easy to hold, well-balanced and not easy to tip. The lip of the glass should be smoothly rounded and comfortable.

# *Table Setting Guide*

## Care of Glassware

- Crystal and glassware often are safer in a dishwasher where a controlled environment exists. The machine can stand hotter water better than human hands.

- If glassware is cleaned in a sink, be sure the sink and rim of faucet are lined with plastic or rubber to avoid chipping or breaking.

- When stacked glasses refuse to be undone, fill the top glass with cold water and put the lower glass in warm water. They will come apart naturally.

- To store glassware, line shelves with several layers of paper or thin sheets of rubber. Place glasses with tops up.

- Glasses should be dried with a lint-free towel. For a higher polish, the glass can be rubbed with tissue paper.

- If a nick in the rim of a glass is very small, it sometimes can be smoothed away with a piece of emery paper.

# Selection and Easy Care

## Glass Making Techniques

**HAND BLOWN:** Hot molten glass is blown into shape on a rod. Swirl on bottom of glass shows where glass was removed from rod.

**MOLD BLOWING:** Expensive molded glass made by glass blown into molds.

**PRESSING:** Inexpensive glass molded by machine. Check for mold marks where the points of a piece were separated for removal of the glass.

**DECORATION:**
  **Coloring:**
    — Finished glass can be painted or stained.
    — Chemicals, such as gold, can be added before glass is melted down to produce ruby glass.
    — Mineral salts added to basic material produces milk glass.
    — Spraying finished glass with colored mixture and then firing produces the iridescent carnival glass.
  **Engraving:** The glass is cut by a small abrasive wheel.
  **Etching:** A design is transferred to glass and etched out by acid.
  **Frosting:** Glass is exposed to acid.
  **Cutting:** Most cut glassware is leaded because the lead gives it strength against the cutter's wheel. Cut crystal is at the top of the expensive line. Some glass and crystal resemble cut glass but the difference can be told by touching the glass. The edge of the cut will be very sharp if hand-cut.

*My favorite patterns . . .*

# Choose Your Glassware

## GLASSWARE

| TYPE | CHARACTERISTICS | PRICE RANGE |
|------|-----------------|-------------|
| LIME GLASS | Made from sand, soda and lime. Lime used for durability, resists scratches. | Inexpensive, machine made. |
| LEAD GLASS | Made from sand, potash and red lead. Lead used for brilliance. Clear ring when tapped. | Expensive because of cost of lead. |

# *Selection and Easy Care*

# Tablecovers and Linens

Table coverings or "linens" are terms used interchangeably to mean tablecloths, mats, runners and napkins. Also included in our discussion are silence cloths.

# Weaves & Designs

**DAMASK:** Originally meant richly designed silk fabric from Damascus. Single damask is tightly woven and will outlast a loosely woven double damask. The pattern in a double damask will stand out clearly. In a single damask, the filling thread passes under one warp thread and over the next four. In a double damask, the filling thread passes under one warp thread and over the next seven or more threads.

**CRASH CLOTH:** A name for plain weave of coarse and uneven yarns, usually cotton, linen or a mixture of fibers. This fabric is often used for luncheon cloths, place mats and napkins.

**LACE:** Usually made of cotton or synthetic fibers. It is best shown off to advantage on a well-cared-for table top finish.

**WOVEN DESIGNS:** Include any design or print made up of fibers woven into a fabric. A structural or colored design shows on both sides of the fabric.

**PRINTED DESIGNS:** Printed on the already woven fabric by hand-block printing, roller printing or screen printing.

# Kinds of Materials Used for Table Coverings

**TABLE COVERINGS**

| TYPE | CHARACTERISTICS | PRICE RANGE |
|------|-----------------|-------------|
| LINEN | Good quality linen has a heavy, leathery feel. Very durable. | expensive |
| COTTON | Fabric may lint unless it has a permanent lint-resistant finish. Quite durable. | moderate to expensive |
| RAYON | Easy to care for. Many table coverings are found with a rayon-polyester fiber combination. | moderate |
| PLASTIC | A thin plastic coating is applied to woven cloth. Easy to care for. | inexpensive |
| OTHERS: CORK, BAMBOO, RAMIE, BURLAP | Found often in place mats. | inexpensive |

## Tablecloth Overhang

Overhang for tablecloths vary between twelve and sixteen inches. The more formal the table, the longer the overhang. Banquet or buffet tables are usually the only tables that have the cloth touching the floor.

## Before You Purchase

Consider these points when purchasing table coverings.
- Color/pattern.
- Fiber content.
- Price.
- Name of manufacturer.
- Ease in cleaning and stain removal.

*My favorite table linens...*

# Table Setting Guide

## Removing Stains

Though today's perma press and stain resistant fabrics keep the care of table top coverings to a minimum, stains still occur. When stains are found, certain procedures should be followed. These procedures are most successful when done as soon as possible after the fact.

**CANDLE WAX:** Remove wax with a knife or fingernail. If it has soaked into material, place stain between paper towels and press with a warm iron. Rotate towel. Sponge back of stained area with nonflammable dry cleaning solvent. Launder.

**COFFEE, CHOCOLATE, TEA, FRUIT:** Rinse 15 minutes in cool water. If stain persists, soak in warm water with enzyme pre-soak. Launder.

**EGG, MILK, CREAM, ICE CREAM:** Sponge with a nonflammable dry cleaning solvent or apply a prewash soil and stain remover. Rinse. Soak 30 minutes or longer in warm water with enzyme pre-soak. Launder.

**LIPSTICK:** Apply nonflammable dry cleaning solvent and blot. Launder.

**WINE:** Do not use soap and water. Permanent discoloration may result. Sprinkle fresh stains immediately with table salt to absorb some of the stain. Sponge the stain promptly with cool water or with club soda if available. Blot thoroughly. Allow to dry.

## Silence Cloth or Table Pad

Using some kind of protective material on the table top not only saves the table from scratches and hot ring marks but also makes meal serving quiet. Felt padding can be purchased by the yard and cut to fit the table or folding table pads can be custom made to fit the shape of the table. Felt on one side and a moisture proof material on the other side helps protect the table from spills. Extra pads can be ordered for the leaves.

## Storage

Storing tablecloths is a perennial problem. The ideal solution is to store the tablecloth with just the center folded. Fold the tablecloth; roll around a cardboard tube or rolled up newspaper and store in a deep linen drawer or cupboard. Use a rod fixed to the inside of a linen closet door as another alternative. In any case make sure the table covers and linens are clean before putting away in storage. Keep good linens which are used infrequently, wrapped in blue paper to prevent yellowing.

# Table Setting Guide

## Place Mats & Runners

Mats should be large enough to hold a place setting but not so large that they overlap each other on the table. Mats can set off a beautiful finished table top. Mats are appropriate alone on a table with or without a runner in the center or placed on a tablecloth. A variety of material is found in mats and depending on the kind of material one can dress the table formally or informally. Place rectangular mats flush with the table or one inch from the table edge. Lay rectangular mats on a round or oval table so that corners touch the table edge. Lay round mats so that they drape partially over table edge.

Mats can be used over tablecloths for a contrast of color, a touch of informality or other desired effect. As with tablecloths, the style of the dinnerware should suggest the style and color of the mat.

Generally speaking, mats are acceptable for every occasion with the exception of afternoon tea or the most formal dining.

Table runners are the newest member of the table covering family. As mentioned, they work well with place mats but can be used alone. When placed on the sides of the table, runners can substitute for place mats or can be used under mats. Try crisscrossing two runners to accommodate four place settings or cross them to form an X in the center of a rectangular table.

Runners, as well, are made of a wide variety of material and are appropriate for all but the most formal of meals. The overhang of runners should be about 15 inches.

# Fancy Folded Napkins

## The Napkin Story

Decorative napkin folding is enjoying a revival in table top decor today. It is interesting to note that napkin folding originated as a craft in the 17th century. You may recall paintings in art museums of young boys bringing steaming dishes to the tables, and on their arms are large towel-sized white cloths used as a kind of community napkin. Each guest was offered the use of this napkin. A cleaning cloth was necessary because forks and spoons were not invented yet. Soon, however, individual napkins were in use and proved practical for the Elizabethan citizens with their elaborate costumes. A very familiar saying originated from this period about stout and goutish men who when trying to tie the ends of the napkin around their necks encountered difficulty in protecting their white pleated collars. The French alluding to this effort laughingly called it "making ends meet." In Italy in the early 16th century, forks and spoons were slowly becoming accepted at the table. Logically then, napkins were no longer needed because the process of eating was, relatively speaking, so much cleaner. However, it wasn't long before napkins came back because of furtive use of the edge of the tablecloth for cleaning purposes. This time napkins were not only used as cleaning tools but as decorative objects.

Giles Rose, master chef of King Charles II, compiled a cookbook for his many cooks and waiters. He included in this book a chapter of 22 different napkin folds. At that time napkins were at least 36 inches square, and of course the napkins had to be that large in order to execute some of the intricate folds created by Giles Rose. These were masterpieces much appreciated by the guest because of the ingenious shapes.

In the Victorian period, a time of elaborate entertaining and dining, decorative napkin folds

# Table Setting Guide

were especially appreciated. The Victorians added a new twist to the art of folded napkins by folding the napkin in such a way as to provide a "cosy" for individual hot rolls. At this time napkins were about 28 inches to 30 inches in size.

Here in America, the Midwest and West were just beginning to have time for the niceties of living; however most of the people were transplanted from their homelands and had few family traditions to rely on. Any printed material on how to manage a home, how to cook a meal, or how to entertain was eagerly sought after. From 1850 to 1900 we find a great number of books published about recipes, etiquette and home management. Napkin folds, of course, were included in this printed literature.

After the early years of 1900, use of fine linens at the dining table slowly became a once in a while practice because of scarcity of labor (don't forget linens were not perma press) and the lack of material during the two World Wars. When people came back from World War II, they settled down to resume a less formal way of living. About this same time, paper products were made available. There were paper towels, paper plates, paper cups and paper napkins. No one had heard of the idea that natural resources wouldn't last forever. And how clean and sanitary, just one wipe with the napkin and throw it away! With the acceptance of paper napkins, the art of folding table napkins became less popular because of the lack of draping quality of the paper napkins.

Even though napkin folding became less popular in America, napkin sculptures were still fashionable for home entertaining in Europe and Canada. In many of these areas napkins are called serviettes. Today, dinner napkins are 18 inches to 22 inches square, luncheon napkins about 17 inches square and tea napkins are 12 inches square.

# *Fancy Folded Napkins*

## Fan • Tas • Tic  Fold

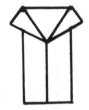

Bring side edge to center; do same with opposite edge.

Fold out top corners.

Roll tightly towards you until you reach the center.

Hold onto roll and accordian pleat rest of the length of the napkin (make pleats size of napkin ring).

Fold roll and pleats in half with the pleats on the outside of fold.

Tuck into napkin ring and set upright.

## Bishop Fold

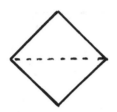

Fold napkin in half to form triangle.

Fold side points to center top point to make a diamond.

Fold across at the dotted line bringing the lower point close to the upper point to form a kind of triangle again.

Fold this same lower point down to bottom of triangle.

Turn napkin over; tuck one point into the other behind the triangle.

Turn napkin again; pull down the two side points, curl and tuck them into napkin. Fold over slightly, the top center point; allow the highest point to remain upright.

## Buffet Pocket Fold

Fold napkin in four parts with open corners at top.

Fold two edges of upper corner down to almost the opposite corner.

Fold the two sides under at dotted lines so they overlap at back.

Place flatware inside the pocket.

## Frilled Fan Fold

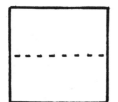

Fold napkin in half.

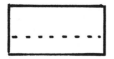

Fold lower edge to one-third of the way from the top.

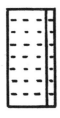

Accordian pleat length of napkin fold.

"Vandyke" lower folded pleated edge by slipping finger between two pleats and pulling the fabric down between the pleats; finger press tightly after each pull.

Arrange in glass.

# Special Care Tips

Most tabletops, tableware, and linen do need a certain amount of attention. Here are some miscellaneous care tips to help keep your possessions looking as good as new.

- Substitute a heavy tablecloth for the felt padding or table protecter commonly used under the tablecloth. If possible add a moistureproof material under the substitute pad to protect the table from spills.

- Make it a rule before you buy new sets of glassware or dinnerware to have a place to store them. A good principle to follow is to give up the same quantity of old, rarely used pieces to make way for the new.

- Rotate the pieces of dinnerware, glassware, and flatware so that all the pieces will show equal amounts of wear or, as in the case of silver, develop the same amount of patina.

- Very inexpensive dinnerware, however well taken care of, has a way of chipping readily, and after a few months you may find yourself eating off of odds and ends or buying a new set. Consider buying a few pieces from a good set of china (buy a set that is labeled "open stock") and fill in when you can.

- Heat china and earthenware in a warm oven only, 150 degrees, unless the ware is ovenware. The glaze on ovenheated ware may craze and the dinnerware sometimes cracks and breaks.

# Table Setting Guide

- Unless the dinnerware specifically states "microwave safe," only put dishes in the microwave for a minute or two for warming.

- Don't scour china, earthenware, or plastic dishes with scouring powder or steel wool as they can be scratched by either method.

- Keep a club soda beverage on hand to remove unexpected spills from tablecloths, clothing, or the rug. Splash the beverage on the stain before it drys and blot until the stain is removed. This method removes wine spills and many other stains.

- When you find yellow spots on your white table linen, it may not be a food or beverage stain but a laundry problem. If a colored liquid detergent is poured directly on white linen in the washing machine, it will sometimes cause yellow spots; particularly if there is polyester in the fabric. All-cotton fabric sometimes will take up a blue stain if a blue liquid detergent is used. You may possibly get the stain out with repeated washings in granular or liquid bluing (a fabric whitener).

- A drop or two of bluing in the rinse water makes glassware glisten.

- Another good product to have on hand is "iron out.™" It's an all purpose rust and stain remover. It will change iron oxide (rust) into a clear soluable state that will flush away.

- Use a chlorine bleach solution for flower vases. This will clean and sanitize most vases.

- For containers that are too narrow for a bottle brush, shake a few spoons of raw rice in a solution of suds.

- De-Solv-it™ removes the sticky residue from sale tags and brand identifications labels. Scratching and scraping time on tableware and accessories is reduced, if not eliminated.

# Special Care Tips

- Brighten coffee makers with a teaspoon of baking soda in the rinse water.

- Clean tea and coffee cups of brown stains by moistening your finger and then dip it in some salt; rub it over the stain.

- If you allow food (mayonnaise for instance) to stay on sterling flatware overnight too many times, you may have problems with rusted or pitted blades.

- Stainless steel flatware can stain if it sits too long in water.

- Pearl, ivory, or horn handles on silver knives or forks should not be allowed to soak in the water or be machine washed. They usually are fastened with cement, which might become loosened.

- Never put rubber bands around wrapped silver because the high sulphur content of rubber will cause tarnish even through the wrappings.

- Don't let the discoloration (tarnish) discourage you. Often a good silver polish and a little polishing will bring the piece back to life.

- When polishing silver, it's best to follow the contour or shape of the piece; don't use a circular motion. Be sure to wash and rinse after using silver polish.

- When all else fails, find a reliable silver plating company. The sentiment of the piece may be well worth the price of having the piece refurbished.

- Don't use boiling water on gold-decorated glassware. Hot water may harm the decorations. If glasses have been in the dishwasher, wait until they have cooled before wiping or handling.

- Drying glassware after washing prevents the cloudiness from water buildup.

- Set glassware upright for storage to prevent nicks in the rim.

# Table Setting Guide

## Table Sense & Manners

Table manners are simply a combination of courtesy and common sense. To know which salad plate is yours without waiting to see what the person seated next to you does is a certain measure of sophistication. This may be an extreme example, but if you've never been told about the proper setting of a table or proper manners at a table, dining can be a nerve-wracking experience.

- A basic rule to remember when you are seated is the napkin on your left is yours. Of course, there's no indecision if the napkin is placed on the plate.

- In answer to which salad plate is yours, the individual serving is always on the left or upper left of the place setting.

- When you are seated, unfold the napkin enough so it can be placed across your lap. Don't completely unfold the napkin and tuck it in your belt.

- After the meal is finished, simply lay the napkin on the table as it happens to fall. It's not necessary to refold it or worse, crumple it into a ball.

- If the dinner party is small, wait until everyone has been served before starting to eat. Buffets are another matter. Here it is proper to eat as soon as you have served yourself.

- It shouldn't have to be mentioned, but for one more time . . . don't talk with your mouth full!

- It also goes without saying, don't take a bite of food when you have just had a drink, and before it is swallowed.

- Another "don't" to remember is not to make a conversational point with the flatware and certainly not to play with the flatware.

# Table Sense & Manners

- As elementary as this may be, learn to eat with your mouth closed. Don't spoil the appetite of the person sitting opposite of you.

- To remove a cherry pit, a fishbone, or anything of that nature from your mouth, simply drop it into a spoon and place the spoon on your plate.

- Most etiquette books say it's not proper to eat French Fries with the fingers but rather to use a fork. Common sense says, if a food can be picked up with a fork . . . use it. On the other hand, if the practice in certain settings, such as fast food establishments or picnics is to eat French Fries with the fingers, then do so.

- When setting the table, know what flatware can be substituted. For example, fruit cocktail can be eaten with teaspoons rather than fruit spoons, seafood appetizers with salad forks, and soup can be eaten with tablespoons instead of soup spoons.

- If bread and butter dishes are used, take a portion of butter and place it on the bread and butter plate with the bread. Don't butter the bread completely, but break off bites of bread as needed and butter only one piece at a time.

- When you stop eating momentarily, place the fork and knife on the plate. A soup spoon is left in the soup bowl or if there is a liner or saucer under the soup bowl, you can rest the spoon there.

- When finger bowls (small bowls of water usually with a flower petal or blossom as decoration) are used, they are served after the end of a particularly sticky course, such as barbecued ribs. Dip your fingers lightly in the water and dry them with your napkin.

- It is only common sense and courtesy to follow the host or hostess in table manners. If the table is not laid exactly as it should be or there is a glitch in the serving of food, quietly follow your host's lead and don't make an issue of the problem. Simply enjoy the hospitality.

# Table Setting Guide

## Wine Service

The study of wine and wine service has been the subject of interest through the ages and many good writings can be found on the subject. Because of the wealth of material, only a few basic facts needed for wine service will be mentioned here. Certainly, if you're interested, pursue the subject further.

- White wines and any sparkling wine like champagne are served from the bottle. You can choose to decant others such as sherry, port, or Madeira.

- "Decanting" simply means to pour from the bottle to a decanter without disturbing the sediment.

- A decanter is a decorative glass bottle, generally with a stopper. It sometimes has a metal tag identifying the contents.

- Some white wines available are Chablis, chardonney, and Sauterne.

- Red wines often chosen are Burgandy, claret, and chianti.

- Port, Madeira, and sweet sherry are classed as sweet dessert wines.

- A white napkin can be wrapped around the wine bottle if desired. It's especially necessary if it's a bottle of red wine, because the napkin will stop any drips from staining the tablecloth.

# Wine Service

- Follow these directions to wrap a napkin around a wine bottle: Fold a square napkin in half; into a triangle. Fold bottom edge of triangle up one quarter and again one quarter. Tie the napkin around the bottle, base of napkin around base of bottle in a simple knot. Turn the bottle so the point of the napkin is facing you. Turn the napkin point down toward the base.

- Always serve wine from the right. Don't pick the glass up from the table to serve.

- It may be a good idea to pour your glass first in case there are any bits of cork to fall into the glass.

- A wine glass should only be half-filled. This is to permit the swirling of wine in the glass and provide room for the wine bouquet (aroma) to circulate.

- A four-ounce stem glass can serve for almost any kind of wine if you must choose one basic glass.

- Most stemware sets are made up of a goblet, wine, and champagne shaped glasses. Other popular stemware pieces are Burgandy, cordials, and brandy glasses.

- It's best to store wine in a dark, dry place preferably at a temperature of about fifty-five degrees.

- Wine bottles should always lie on their side because the corks need to be kept damp to prevent skrinkage.

- Red wines are served at room temperature. White wine and any sparkling wine (Champagne) may be chilled or iced.

- Set stemmed glassware in a triangle, in a row, straight across, or in a diagonal line. Begin with the largest glass to the left just above the table knife tip. In a triangle, set the small glass in front, or in a row, grade the glasses down according to their height.

# Table Setting Guide

## Table Setting Possibilities

Where and how you set a table is always important to the dining occasion. An unexpected or "just right" setting will elicit delighted reactions from your guests. The following is a sampling of possible tablescapes for a variety of tabletop situations.

- Change the routine placement of four place settings, one on each side, on a rectangular table. Instead, place two settings on each long side of the table. This does away with the stiff head of the table feeling. Balance the head and foot of the table with two small decorative pieces, one at either end.

- Solve the seating problem of a large table when you plan an intimate dinner for two. Lay a place setting at the head of the table and one place setting just to the left or right side of the table. Avoid setting the second cover at the middle of the side unless the table is a small square.

- Another way to achieve a setting for two is to slide the table next to the wall. Place two place settings side by side for an intimate dining experience. When the table is set only on one side, restore the balance by setting a large floral centerpiece on the "vacant" side or hang a decorative picture on the wall. Coordinate the table appointments to the picture.

- Moving to an outside table setting, embellish the lawn umbrella table with two semi-circular flower containers around the handle of the umbrella. Choose flowers that will compliment the color scheme of the table setting.

- Dress up a less than perfect table, such as a card table, with richly colored tablecloths. Plan the size of the tablecloth so it will hang to the floor,

# Table Setting Possibilities

thereby hiding the unattractive legs of the card table. Coordinate chair covers and the tablecloth. Patterns for chair covers are available from your favorite dress pattern companies.

- A small round table with a setting of three can look balanced if you move the centerpiece to the "vacant" side of the table. Let round placemats hang slightly over the edge of the table.

- Use the sideboard, set with serving dishes of the main dish and salad, as an invitation for the guests to help themselves. Set vases of tall flowers to stand at each end of the sideboard to complete the setting. Do have the dining table ready and set with the appropriate dinnerware.

- Place the buffet setting diagonally on the table which not only gives it unexpected eye-appeal but gives more room (at one corner) to the guests who may want it for laying down an occasional plate.

- Glass tabletops are most effective when placemats or runners are used. Tablecloths can be used but they do cover the charm of the glass. When choosing placemats, select mats large enough so there is adequate room for all the dinnerware pieces. This will cut down on noise and clatter. The napkins are laid on the glass top alongside the placemat.

- The eating bar of the kitchen counter can be set as the buffet center. Informal linens and tableware rather than silver, china, and damask will complement the setting better. Runners or placemats casually draped on the surface are background enough.

- Some table styles dictate the kind of tableware used. For example, trestle tables make a lovely background for country or traditional tabletop settings. Glass topped tables can accommodate formal traditional ware as well as contempory casual. Country settings, though, tend to look out of place on most glass table tops.

# Table Setting Guide

## Flower Talk

Flowers are often considered essential when setting a special table. To be sure, there are methods and tricks of the trade that will create a successful flower arrangement. But, the best advice is to simply enjoy fussing with the arrangement until you're satisfied.

- The centerpiece should never block the view of the guests on one side of the table from those on the other side. However, you can sparsely group long-stemmed flowers, or place two vases apart from each other and near the ends of the table top to raise the flowers above the eye level and leave an open center space.

- Using only one color in a floral bouquet can be interesting if the flowers are different in size, shape, and texture.

- When choosing flowers for an arrangement, remember there should be one major ruling color for the table setting. Emphasize the ruling color in the floral arrangement.

- As you are arranging flowers, keep in mind's eye the mass or shape of the arrangement. The flowers may be roughly arranged to form a rectangle, a circle or a part of one, or a triangle.

- To keep the arrangement fresh longer, be sure to cut off foliage below the water line. Also, diagonally cut the stems rather than having the stems crushed against the bottom of the container so they can absorb more water.

- Dried flowers will last almost forever with an occasional freshening. For such arrangements use rustic containers such as woven baskets, metal containers, or rough pottery.

# *Flower Talk*

- Simple green leaves, skillfully arranged, make an effective centerpiece. Select leaves that are different in size, shape, texture, and shine. Green foliage and off-white candles are a wonderful combination.

- In some cases, an individual centerpiece placed at each place setting is more effective then one large centerpiece. Choose from miniature bouquets in containers, or one blossom, like a rose or hibiscus, simply laid on each place setting.

- The variety of containers for individual centerpieces makes decorating the table easy. Juice glasses, stemmed glasses, seashells, even thimbles that can hold tiny violets offer interesting possibilities.

- Use shallow containers, such as finger bowls, for floating fresh flower petals or blossoms.

- For a late summer bounty centerpiece, layer dried flower petals, one color on top of another, in a deep, glass cylindrical vase or salad bowl.

- Potted flowers, either one large pot or three small pots grouped together on a tray, make a quick but definite statement on the table.

- If the flowers in the centerpiece are at the peak of their perfection the night before, store the centerpiece in the refrigerator to hold their perfection until just before the arrival of the guests.

- To keep flower stems in place, choose from metal or plastic frogs, marbles (clear or in any color), pebbles or stones, or florist foam blocks.

- When the color scheme is vital, take a plate or napkin that closely resembles the color with you before buying the flowers. If a theme such as an Oriental party or a time-inspired party is foremost, take a relevant object with you.

# Table Setting Guide

## The Party Aid Duties

An extra pair of hands or two is essential when giving teas, receptions, luncheons, and dinners with a large guest list. The following tips show how the temporary party aid can help to ensure a smoothly run party.

- Before the party, make out a list of tabletop needs such as napkins, flowers, party favors, name cards, or centerpiece accessories.

- Cover the table with a table protector and tablecloth. Iron any wrinkles and creases except the middle lengthwise crease beforehand.

- Set the table and arrange the centerpiece. If candles will be used, light them before the guests are seated.

- Arrange the dessert dishes and flatware in preparation of serving the dessert.

- Fold the napkins oblong, square, or in intricate sculptures and set them in place at each placesetting.

- Serve the hostess first (or the guest of honor if the hostess requests).

- Next, serve the person to the right, and on around the table to the right.

- Place and remove dishes from the left with the left hand.

- Serve and remove beverages from the right with the right hand.

- Fill water glasses three-fourth full. Do not lift glasses. Fill all-purpose wine glasses one-half full for dinner wines and one-fourth full for appetizer and dessert wines.

# The Party Aid Duties

- Hold a clean napkin in the left hand when pouring beverages, to catch any drops.

- When passing a serving platter or bread tray, hold it low and near the guest, in the left hand, steadying with the right.

- Place handles of serving tools on the serving platter toward the guest. If necessary, rearrange food to look attractive for each guest.

- Use a clean folded napkin to protect the hand from hot platters and serving dishes.

- If a dish is being removed and replaced with another at the same time, remove with the right hand and replace with the left.

- If drinks have been served in another room, try to find time during dinner to pick up the used glasses and napkins and to empty ash trays.

- Before dessert is served, remove serving dishes and flatware first, then remove guest's dishes and silver. Everything except glassware and decorations should be taken from the table.

- Salad and bread and butter plates may be removed together. Lift salad with right and bread and butter with the left hand.

- Remove crumbs from the left before serving dessert. Brush them with a folded napkin or crumb brush into a small tray or plate held just below the table edge.

- While guests are enjoying dessert, make coffee and arrange the tray for demitasse service.

- Serve dessert and coffee (unless demitasse is being served later in the living room).

- While guests serve themselves from the buffet, remove used glasses and napkins if cocktails were served. Empty and replace ash trays.

# Table Setting Guide

- After guests have served themselves from the buffet and are seated with their plates, serve hot bread and beverage, if needed.

- Rearrange and pass platters of food from the buffet. Refill beverage glasses.

- Avoid reaching across or passing in front of guests. Keep ash trays emptied.

- When guests have finished at the buffet service, remove plates and serve dessert.

- Serve coffee, cream, and sugar; or bring the tray for demitasse service after the buffet dessert plates have been removed.

# Tablecloth Size Chart

| Shape | Table Sizes | Cloth | Persons Seated |
|---|---|---|---|
| SQUARE | 28" to 40" | 52" x 52" | 4 |
| ROUND | 30" to 42" diameter | 52" round | 4 |
| | 42" to 44" diameter | 60" to 68" | 4 to 6 |
| | 42" to 54" diameter | 68" w/fringe | 6 |
| | 42" to 60" diameter | 72" round | 6 |
| | 64" to 76" diameter | 90" round | 6 to 8 |
| OBLONG | 28" x 46" to 36" x 54" | 52" x 70" | 4 to 6 |
| | 36" x 56" to 42" x 62" | 60" x 80" | 6 to 8 |
| | 42" x 60" to 48" x 72" | 72" x 90" | 6 to 8 |
| | 42" x 72" to 48" x 90" | 72" x 108" | 8 to 10 |
| OVAL | 28" x 46" to 36" x 54" | 52" x 70" | 4 to 6 |
| | 36" x 56" to 42" x 62" | 60" x 80" | 6 to 8 |
| | 42" x 60" to 48" x 72" | 72" x 90" | 6 to 8 |
| | 42" x 72" to 48" x 90" | 72" x 108" | 8 to 10 |

*Recommended by the Linen Trade Association.*

# Index

Sharon Dlugosch, freelance home economist, is the author of several books including the best selling "Folding Table Napkins," and "Tabletop Vignettes." She has also written several one-of-a-kind party and wedding theme books.

This handbook is her timely response to the growing trend toward dining-in and home entertainment. She draws from her extensive experience conducting workshops and giving demonstrations to present this easily readable guide anyone can understand and use.

## Available from Brighton Publications, Inc. . . .

*Folding Table Napkins: A New Look at a Traditional Craft* by Sharon Dlugosch

*Table Setting Guide, Newly Revised* by Sharon Dlugosch

*Tabletop Vignettes* by Sharon Dlugosch

*Wedding Plans: 50 Unique Themes for the Wedding of Your Dreams* by Sharon Dlugosch

*Wedding Hints & Reminders* by Sharon Dlugosch

*Wedding Occasions: 101 New Party Themes for Wedding Showers, Rehearsal Dinners, Engagement Parties, and More!* by Cynthia Lueck Sowden

*Games for Wedding Shower Fun* by Sharon Dlugosch, Florence Nelson

*Baby Shower Fun* by Sharon Dlugosch

*Games for Baby Shower Fun* by Sharon Dlugosch

These books are available in selected stores and catalogs. If you're having trouble finding these books in your area send a self-addressed, stamped business-size envelope to Brighton Publications, Inc., P.O. Box 12706, New Brighton, MN 55112, and request ordering information.